Grokking LLM: From Fundamentals to Advanced Techniques in Large

Language Models

Contents

Introduction to Large Language Models (LLMs)

What are LLMs?

Large Language Models (LLMs) are a class of artificial intelligence models designed to understand and generate human language. They are built using deep learning techniques and are capable of performing a wide range of language-related tasks, such as translation, summarization, text generation, and more. LLMs like GPT-3 and GPT-4 have millions to billions of parameters, enabling them to generate coherent and contextually relevant text based on the input they receive.

Evolution of Language Models

The development of language models has progressed significantly over the past few decades. Early models relied on rule-based systems and statistical methods. The introduction of neural networks and deep learning marked a major shift, with models like word2vec and GloVe providing better word embeddings. The advent of Transformer architecture, introduced by Vaswani et al. in 2017, revolutionized the field, leading to the development of powerful models such as BERT, GPT, and T5.

Applications of LLMs

LLMs have a broad range of applications across various domains:

- **Text Generation:** Creating human-like text for chatbots, content creation, and storytelling.

- **Translation:** Translating text from one language to another with high accuracy.

- **Summarization:** Condensing long documents into shorter, coherent summaries.

- **Question Answering:** Providing accurate answers to user queries based on context.

- **Sentiment Analysis:** Analyzing the sentiment or emotion expressed in a piece of text.

- **Conversational AI:** Building intelligent virtual assistants and chatbots for customer service and other applications.

Ethical Considerations (brief overview)

The deployment of LLMs raises several ethical issues, including:

- **Bias and Fairness:** LLMs can inherit and amplify biases present in the training data, leading to unfair or discriminatory outcomes.

- **Privacy:** The use of large datasets for training can pose privacy risks if sensitive information is inadvertently included.

- **Misinformation:** The ability of LLMs to generate realistic text can be misused to spread false information.

- **Accountability:** Determining responsibility for the outputs generated by LLMs can be challenging, especially when they are integrated into critical decision-making processes.

Fundamentals of Language Models

Basic Concepts in Natural Language Processing (NLP)

NLP involves the interaction between computers and human language. Key concepts include:

- **Syntax and Semantics:** Understanding the structure and meaning of sentences.

- **Tokenization:** Breaking down text into individual words or tokens.

- **Part-of-Speech Tagging:** Identifying the grammatical roles of words in a sentence.

- **Named Entity Recognition (NER):** Detecting and classifying entities like names, dates, and locations in text.

Overview of Neural Networks

Neural networks are the backbone of modern language models. They consist of layers of interconnected nodes (neurons) that process input data to produce output. Key types include:

- **Feedforward Neural Networks:** The simplest type, where connections do not form cycles.

- **Recurrent Neural Networks (RNNs):** Designed for sequential data, with connections that loop back.

- **Convolutional Neural Networks (CNNs):** Effective for spatial data, often used in image processing.

- **Transformer Networks:** Utilize self-attention mechanisms to process input data in parallel, crucial for modern LLMs.

Introduction to Transformer Architecture

Transformers, introduced in the paper "Attention Is All You Need," have become the foundation of LLMs. Key components include:

- **Self-Attention Mechanism:** Allows the model to weigh the importance of different words in a sentence, capturing dependencies regardless of their distance.

- **Multi-Head Attention:** Enhances the model's ability to focus on different parts of the input simultaneously.

- **Positional Encoding:** Injects information about the position of words in a sentence, as Transformers do not inherently consider order.

- **Encoder-Decoder Structure:** Typically used in tasks like translation, where the encoder processes the input and the decoder generates the output.

Building Blocks of LLMs

Tokens and Tokenization

Tokenization is the process of breaking down text into smaller units, called tokens. These can be words, subwords, or characters. Effective tokenization is crucial for model performance, as it impacts how well the model can learn and represent language. Subword tokenization methods, like Byte Pair Encoding (BPE) and WordPiece, are commonly used in LLMs to handle rare words and morphological variations.

Embeddings

Embeddings are dense vector representations of tokens that capture their meanings and relationships in a continuous vector space. They allow the model to understand semantic similarities between words. Common embedding techniques include:

- **Word Embeddings:** Represent words as fixed-length vectors, e.g., word2vec, GloVe.
- **Contextual Embeddings:** Generate dynamic representations based on the context of the word in a sentence, e.g., BERT embeddings.

Attention Mechanism

The attention mechanism is a key innovation in modern NLP models, enabling them to focus on relevant parts of the input when generating output. It assigns different weights to different tokens in the input sequence, allowing the model to capture long-range dependencies and improve translation, summarization, and other tasks.

Positional Encoding

Since Transformers do not have an inherent sense of order, positional encoding is used to provide information about the positions of tokens in the input sequence. These encodings are added to the token embeddings, allowing the model to distinguish between different positions and capture the structure of the input text. Positional encodings can be learned or fixed, with sine and cosine functions commonly used in fixed positional encodings.

Popular Large Language Models

GPT-3 and GPT-4

GPT-3 (Generative Pre-trained Transformer 3) and GPT-4 are among the most well-known large language models developed by OpenAI. These models are built on the Transformer architecture and are trained on diverse datasets containing a vast amount of text from the internet.

- **GPT-3:** With 175 billion parameters, GPT-3 can generate highly coherent and contextually relevant text, perform complex language tasks, and even solve some reasoning problems. It excels in tasks such as text completion, translation, summarization, and question answering.

- **GPT-4:** The successor to GPT-3, GPT-4 further improves on its predecessor with more parameters, enhanced training techniques, and better performance across various NLP tasks. It offers improved understanding, more accurate text generation, and greater adaptability to different contexts and applications.

BERT and its Variants

BERT (Bidirectional Encoder Representations from Transformers) is another groundbreaking model developed by Google. Unlike GPT, which is primarily a generative model, BERT is designed for understanding and interpreting text.

- **BERT:** Trained using a bidirectional approach, BERT considers the context from both directions (left-to-right and right-to-left) to provide a deeper understanding of language. It has achieved state-of-the-art results on a range of NLP tasks, including question answering and named entity recognition.

- **Variants:** Various adaptations of BERT have been developed to enhance its performance and adapt it to specific tasks. These include RoBERTa (Robustly optimized BERT approach), DistilBERT (a smaller and faster version), and ALBERT (A Lite BERT).

T5 and Other Models

T5 (Text-To-Text Transfer Transformer) is a versatile model developed by Google that converts all NLP tasks into a text-to-text format. This unified approach allows T5 to be applied to a wide range of tasks using the same model.

- **T5:** Capable of tasks such as translation, summarization, and classification by treating them as text generation problems, T5 has demonstrated impressive performance across various benchmarks.

- **Other Models:** In addition to T5, other notable models include XLNet (which combines the best aspects of BERT and autoregressive models), ERNIE (enhanced representation through knowledge integration), and ELECTRA (efficiently learning an encoder that classifies token replacements accurately).

Comparative Analysis of LLMs

When comparing different large language models, several factors should be considered:

- **Architecture:** Differences in architecture, such as GPT's autoregressive approach versus BERT's bidirectional training, impact their suitability for different tasks.

- **Performance:** Evaluation on benchmark datasets and real-world applications provides insights into the strengths and weaknesses of each model.

- **Parameter Size:** Larger models generally offer better performance but come with increased computational costs and resource requirements.

- **Adaptability:** The ease with which a model can be fine-tuned for specific tasks and its ability to generalize across different domains are crucial considerations.

Training Large Language Models

Data Collection and Preprocessing

The quality and diversity of training data are critical for the performance of large language models. Data collection involves sourcing large datasets from various domains, ensuring they cover a wide range of topics and language uses.

- **Preprocessing:** This step includes cleaning the data, removing noise, handling missing values, and tokenizing the text. Effective preprocessing ensures the model learns from high-quality and relevant data, reducing the risk of overfitting and improving generalization.

Training Objectives and Loss Functions

Training large language models involves defining appropriate objectives and loss functions to guide the learning process.

- **Training Objectives:** Common objectives include masked language modeling (used in BERT) and autoregressive modeling (used in GPT). These objectives determine how the model predicts missing or next words based on the context.

- **Loss Functions:** The choice of loss function impacts how the model updates its parameters during training. Cross-entropy loss is commonly used for language models, measuring the difference between predicted and actual distributions.

Fine-Tuning Techniques

Fine-tuning allows a pre-trained model to adapt to specific tasks or domains, enhancing its performance.

- **Transfer Learning:** Pre-trained models are fine-tuned on task-specific data with additional training steps, often requiring fewer resources and less data than training from scratch.

- **Domain Adaptation:** Fine-tuning on data from a particular domain (e.g., medical texts) improves the model's ability to handle domain-specific language and tasks.

Handling Bias and Ensuring Fairness

Addressing bias in large language models is crucial for ensuring fairness and avoiding harmful outcomes.

- **Bias Mitigation:** Techniques such as data augmentation, adversarial training, and fairness constraints help reduce biases in the model.

- **Fairness Assessment:** Regular evaluation of model outputs for bias and fairness, using metrics and benchmarks, helps identify and address potential issues.

Fine-Tuning Large Language Models for Domain-Specific Applications

Fine-tuning large language models (LLMs) for specific domains is essential for maximizing their effectiveness in specialized applications. Unlike general-purpose training, fine-tuning allows LLMs to excel in environments with unique linguistic conventions, terminology, and expectations. In this chapter, we'll explore advanced methods for fine-tuning large models to adapt them to diverse domains, such as healthcare, finance, and legal sectors. This process involves intricate adjustments, including data preparation techniques, transfer learning, and methods for continuous adaptation. Through real-world examples and best practices, this chapter will provide insights into enhancing the relevance and performance of LLMs in targeted fields.

Fine-tuning begins with a thorough understanding of the domain itself. The data used for fine-tuning must reflect the specialized language and contextual depth of the target domain. For instance, the medical field contains complex terminology and specific ways of presenting information, while legal language is structured and formulaic, requiring a model to understand nuanced phrasing. Selecting and curating data that authentically represents these characteristics forms the foundation of successful domain adaptation. Additionally, data preprocessing steps such as tokenization and text normalization need to be re-evaluated, as the meaning of certain terms may differ from general usage or require unique handling for accurate representation.

To start the fine-tuning process, data curation becomes the first major task. High-quality, domain-specific datasets are crucial; even seemingly minor discrepancies can affect model performance. The dataset might come from publicly available sources, proprietary databases, or a combination. For example, to create a healthcare LLM, clinical notes, research articles, and electronic health records (EHRs) could be essential components of the dataset. The goal is to capture not just vocabulary but the unique structure and contextual nuance within the domain's content. In practice, organizations may need to prioritize specific sources that meet regulatory or quality standards, especially when dealing with confidential or sensitive information.

Once the data is collected, preprocessing takes on an essential role. Tokenization for domain-specific language can be particularly challenging because specialized terms might be divided incorrectly by standard tokenizers. Subword tokenization, which segments words into smaller parts, may not recognize medical compounds or legal phrases as cohesive units. One way to address this issue is to employ customized tokenizers trained on domain data to retain the integrity of specialized terms. Another approach is dictionary-based tokenization, where predefined vocabulary lists from the domain ensure consistent handling of technical terms.

A key step in domain-specific fine-tuning is transfer learning, a method that leverages knowledge from general-purpose models to enhance performance in specific areas. Transfer learning allows LLMs to retain core linguistic and syntactic knowledge acquired during general training while adapting to the nuances of the new domain. Transfer learning can be divided into two major approaches: feature-based transfer and fine-tuning transfer. Feature-based transfer involves extracting high-level features from a general model and feeding them into a smaller model fine-tuned for the specific task. In contrast, fine-tuning transfer involves directly adjusting the weights of the LLM to improve its accuracy and performance in the target domain.

In the feature-based transfer approach, the main goal is to identify key linguistic features that remain relevant in the domain-specific application. For example, certain syntactic structures and grammar rules are universally applicable, regardless of the domain. By retaining these foundational aspects and focusing on domain-specific vocabulary and usage patterns, the model becomes more versatile and effective for the new context. However, feature-based transfer has its limitations, especially in highly specialized areas where deeper semantic understanding is necessary.

Fine-tuning transfer, which directly updates the model's weights, tends to yield better results in domain-specific applications. This approach involves further training of the LLM using labeled data from the domain, enabling it to learn specific associations, relationships, and knowledge relevant to that field. For instance, in healthcare applications, the model can learn to prioritize certain phrases, recognize medical abbreviations, and interpret context-specific meanings of general words. This approach is especially effective when there are abundant labeled data, as it allows the model to generalize within the domain while maintaining high accuracy.

Hyperparameter tuning is another critical component of fine-tuning. Standard hyperparameters, such as learning rate, batch size, and the number of training epochs, require careful adjustment to optimize the model's performance in the target domain. Choosing an appropriate learning rate, for instance, can prevent the model from "forgetting" the foundational language skills it learned during pre-training while still allowing it to specialize. Similarly, batch size adjustments can influence the model's ability to generalize. Smaller batch sizes can help maintain the nuance of the domain-specific data, whereas larger batch sizes may lead to oversimplified generalizations.

To evaluate the effectiveness of the fine-tuning process, specialized metrics should be used alongside general evaluation metrics like accuracy, precision, and recall. Domain-specific metrics provide deeper insights into a model's success in interpreting context, accuracy in terminology, and adherence to domain conventions. For example, in a legal language model, measuring clause accuracy and the model's ability to handle conditional statements may be more relevant than traditional language metrics. Healthcare models may be evaluated based on their ability to identify relationships between symptoms and diagnoses, a metric beyond conventional natural language processing (NLP) evaluation standards.

One advanced strategy to improve the quality of domain-specific LLMs is continual learning, which enables the model to stay updated with the latest information from the field. Continual learning allows LLMs to adapt without requiring complete retraining, making it ideal for rapidly evolving domains such as medicine, where new discoveries are constantly published. In a continual learning setting, data from recent developments are incrementally incorporated into the model, updating its knowledge base while preserving prior learning. This approach requires careful balance: without fine control, the model risks losing valuable knowledge, a phenomenon known as catastrophic forgetting.

To mitigate catastrophic forgetting, various strategies can be employed. One popular technique is Elastic Weight Consolidation (EWC), which prevents important weights from shifting too drastically by penalizing changes to specific parameters during training. Another approach is regularization, where previously learned knowledge is periodically revisited to reinforce prior understanding. These techniques can be integrated into the fine-tuning process to ensure a balanced, robust model.

Additionally, reinforcement learning offers promising opportunities for further specialization. In a reinforcement learning setup, the model interacts with a simulated environment to refine its responses based on feedback. For example, a healthcare LLM could be trained to prioritize certain answers based on simulated doctor-patient interactions, improving its decision-making and communication style. Reinforcement learning is especially useful in applications that require nuanced judgment, where conventional training falls short. By adjusting model behavior according to reward signals, reinforcement learning can drive LLMs towards more contextually appropriate responses.

When fine-tuning LLMs for sensitive domains like healthcare and legal applications, ethical considerations become paramount. Domain-specific LLMs must be transparent, unbiased, and respectful of privacy requirements. In healthcare, for instance, patient confidentiality and HIPAA compliance must be strictly maintained. Legal models require similar rigor to ensure they don't inadvertently offer biased or unethical advice. Fine-tuning processes should include strategies to mitigate bias, such as data balancing and fairness assessments. Ensuring that the model adheres to ethical standards while delivering accurate information is not only a best practice but a legal and ethical obligation.

Post-deployment monitoring is essential to maintain the relevance and accuracy of fine-tuned LLMs. Even after the model is integrated into an application, regular performance evaluations are necessary to detect any degradation in quality. Techniques like model drift detection and retraining alerts enable continuous monitoring and maintenance of model performance. In high-stakes fields, model drift can have severe consequences, so early detection and prompt updates are necessary to maintain reliability. Alerts can be based on user feedback, statistical changes in predictions, or shifts in data distribution.

Moreover, user feedback can be a valuable source of data for ongoing model improvement. Feedback loops allow developers to capture real-world input that might not be available during initial fine-tuning. Incorporating feedback into the model's fine-tuning cycle strengthens its adaptability, allowing it to meet evolving needs more effectively. This approach is particularly valuable in customer service applications, where user interactions provide insights into the model's effectiveness and areas for improvement.

Finally, organizations deploying domain-specific LLMs need to establish a robust governance framework. This includes monitoring policies for data privacy, regular audits for bias detection, and transparency mechanisms to explain model behavior. Governance frameworks provide clarity and accountability, helping organizations ensure their models remain aligned with legal and ethical standards over time. In some industries, governance frameworks may also be legally mandated, making it essential for developers and business leaders to stay informed about regulatory changes.

Optimizing Large Language Models for Real-Time Performance

Optimizing large language models (LLMs) for real-time applications poses unique challenges. These models are often computationally intensive and demand significant resources, which can lead to high latency. However, for real-time use cases, such as conversational AI, recommendation systems, or real-time content moderation, rapid response times are critical to ensuring a smooth user experience. In this chapter, we'll explore advanced techniques for improving LLM efficiency, including model pruning, quantization, knowledge distillation, and adaptive computation. We'll also discuss hardware optimization strategies and best practices for balancing model performance with latency, throughput, and energy efficiency.

The foundation of optimizing LLMs for real-time performance lies in understanding the model's architecture and identifying bottlenecks that lead to latency. Transformers, the architecture behind most LLMs, use attention mechanisms that can become resource-intensive as the model scales. For real-time optimization, breaking down the model into its essential components—such as encoder, decoder, and attention layers—helps identify where most computation occurs and what can be streamlined. Typically, attention layers consume the most resources, especially in tasks that involve long input sequences. By applying selective optimizations, we can target these areas without sacrificing too much accuracy.

Model pruning is one of the most widely used techniques to reduce model size and complexity. In LLMs, pruning eliminates non-essential neurons and weights, focusing computation on the most relevant parts of the model. There are several approaches to pruning, including weight pruning, neuron pruning, and structured pruning. Weight pruning involves zeroing out low-magnitude weights that contribute minimally to the model's output. Neuron pruning, on the other hand, targets specific neurons in the network that have limited impact on final predictions. Structured pruning takes this further by removing entire layers or attention heads, achieving greater reductions in model size and computational cost.

Quantization is another valuable technique that converts a model's weights and activations from high-precision (e.g., 32-bit floating point) to lower-precision representations (e.g., 8-bit integers). Quantization achieves significant reductions in both memory and computation requirements without substantial loss of accuracy. There are two main types of quantization: static and dynamic. Static quantization involves pre-converting weights and activations before deployment, whereas dynamic quantization adjusts during runtime, depending on the input. This latter approach is particularly beneficial in applications where accuracy needs to be preserved with minimal quantization-induced errors.

Knowledge distillation is an advanced optimization technique in which a smaller "student" model learns to mimic the behavior of a larger "teacher" model. During this process, the teacher model's predictions are used to train the student model, which is then deployed in real-time environments due to its reduced size and complexity. The student model learns not only to replicate the teacher model's predictions but also to interpret nuanced relationships within the data. This approach allows developers to deploy highly efficient models with minimal loss of performance, making it ideal for real-time applications. Knowledge distillation is especially effective in scenarios where the student model can still capture essential domain-specific knowledge from the teacher model.

Another optimization method for real-time performance is adaptive computation, where the model dynamically adjusts its processing complexity based on input requirements. This approach leverages the fact that not every input requires the full computational power of the LLM. In a real-time chatbot application, for example, simple responses to basic questions may not require the model to utilize all its layers or parameters. Adaptive computation dynamically decides which parts of the model to engage based on input complexity, minimizing latency and maximizing efficiency. Techniques such as layer skipping or conditional computation can be used to implement this approach, selectively activating only necessary parts of the model.

In addition to model-level optimizations, hardware selection plays a critical role in achieving real-time performance. Specialized hardware, such as GPUs, TPUs, or even AI-specific accelerators, significantly reduces latency. Each hardware type has its strengths: GPUs excel in parallel processing, making them ideal for batch operations, while TPUs are optimized for TensorFlow operations and can be particularly effective in cloud environments. Moreover, AI-specific chips, such as the NVIDIA A100 or Google's TPU v4, provide low-latency processing tailored to large-scale models. Selecting the right hardware, combined with optimizing configurations, enables LLMs to operate within real-time constraints.

To further enhance real-time efficiency, inference batching is a practical technique used to process multiple inputs simultaneously. Rather than executing each request independently, batching consolidates multiple queries into a single pass, reducing redundancy and latency. However, in low-latency applications, finding the right batch size is essential—too large, and the model risks increased wait times; too small, and it may miss out on efficiency gains. Dynamic batching, which adjusts batch size in real-time based on incoming request rates, provides an effective solution, allowing models to remain responsive during fluctuating demand.

Another hardware-optimized strategy is leveraging sparse matrices to store weights, which reduces memory requirements and accelerates computation by focusing only on relevant data. Sparse representations become particularly effective in environments where hardware is optimized for sparse computations, such as certain GPUs and AI accelerators. By converting dense matrices into sparse formats, unnecessary calculations are minimized, and model speed is significantly enhanced. Combining sparse representations with quantization and pruning can yield powerful results, making it a foundational approach in latency-sensitive applications.

Beyond model and hardware optimizations, model caching is an effective approach for scenarios with repeated or similar queries. For example, in a chatbot application, commonly asked questions can be cached, allowing the system to retrieve precomputed responses instantly. By caching results, organizations can serve repeated queries with minimal processing, preserving model resources for unique and complex queries. However, cache invalidation remains a challenge—keeping the cache updated to reflect changes in the underlying model or knowledge base requires careful design and periodic refreshes.

In real-time systems, monitoring latency metrics and identifying bottlenecks is vital for continuous optimization. Real-time applications benefit from monitoring tools that track latency at multiple levels—model inference time, data retrieval, and network latency—to provide insights into areas needing improvement. Optimizations may include tuning hyperparameters, increasing hardware resources, or adjusting model components. Dynamic monitoring also allows the system to scale up or down based on traffic patterns, helping maintain consistent performance while controlling costs.

By combining model optimizations, adaptive computation, efficient hardware, and strategic monitoring, real-time applications of LLMs can be realized with significant performance improvements. The strategies outlined here enable LLMs to function within the strict demands of real-time systems, ensuring seamless and efficient user experiences without compromising model accuracy or relevance.

Integrating Multimodal Capabilities into Large Language Models

As AI applications become more complex, there's a growing demand to integrate multimodal capabilities into large language models (LLMs). Multimodal LLMs can process and analyze diverse types of data—text, images, audio, and even video—enabling more comprehensive and context-aware interactions. For applications like interactive customer service, medical diagnostics, or autonomous driving, where multiple data sources inform decision-making, multimodal LLMs offer substantial advantages. In this chapter, we'll explore techniques for building and fine-tuning multimodal models, strategies for data fusion, and methods to optimize these models for real-world applications.

The integration of multimodal capabilities begins with understanding how to combine multiple data streams effectively. Traditional LLMs are optimized for text, relying on tokenized input representations. However, adding visual or auditory input necessitates a different representation format. For example, images might be represented as pixel arrays or features extracted from convolutional layers, while audio is often processed as spectrograms or waveforms. Combining these formats with language tokens requires advanced fusion techniques, such as co-attention mechanisms or cross-modal transformers, which allow models to process disparate inputs as cohesive information.

One primary approach to integrating multiple modalities is cross-modal training, where models learn to map different data types into a shared latent space. In a shared latent space, text, images, and audio features can interact, making it easier for the model to recognize relationships between them. For instance, a model could associate an image of a stethoscope with medical terminology, improving its ability to answer healthcare-related queries. Cross-modal transformers enable this integration by using parallel encoders for each modality that feed into a shared decoder, synthesizing multimodal information into a unified response.

A critical step in multimodal training is selecting the right datasets to capture meaningful correlations across modalities. For example, in training a medical diagnostic model, combining text data from medical literature with images from diagnostic imaging datasets improves the model's ability to associate visual symptoms with medical terminology. Unlike single-modality models, multimodal models require datasets with aligned text and visual or auditory elements. However, collecting aligned datasets can be challenging. Synthetic data generation, where images and text are artificially aligned, can help address this issue, creating a more balanced dataset that reflects multimodal interactions.

Data fusion techniques are essential for combining inputs from various modalities without overloading the model. Early fusion combines data at the input level, embedding text and images before they enter the model. While simple, early fusion can lead to increased complexity and memory demands. Late fusion, by contrast, processes each modality independently and then combines their outputs, providing a more modular approach that preserves individual modality characteristics. Dynamic fusion, a more advanced approach, allows the model to choose which modalities to prioritize based on context, optimizing for flexibility and interpretability.

Once the data fusion strategy is selected, attention mechanisms become vital for integrating multimodal information. Co-attention mechanisms, for instance, allow the model to align text tokens with image features, enhancing its ability to relate words to visual elements. For instance, in a customer service setting, co-attention could allow a model to link a product image with descriptive text, enabling it to answer queries about specific product details. Co-attention mechanisms improve the interpretability and robustness of multimodal models, making them more effective in real-world applications.

Self-supervised learning (SSL) is another powerful technique for training multimodal models. SSL enables models to learn from unlabeled data, which is abundant for certain modalities, such as image or video data. During SSL, the model generates its training objectives, such as predicting a masked text segment based on an image, which helps it learn cross-modal relationships without explicit supervision. Self-supervised multimodal models, such as those using BERT-style training objectives for both text and image segments, can capture complex relationships that improve performance across multiple tasks.

Evaluating multimodal models requires unique metrics and benchmarks that assess cross-modal performance. Traditional NLP metrics like accuracy and F1 scores must be augmented with vision metrics, such as mean average precision (mAP) for object detection tasks. Cross-modal benchmarks, such as the Visual Question Answering (VQA) dataset or the Audio-Visual Scene-Aware Dialog (AVSD) dataset, are specifically designed for multimodal evaluation. Effective evaluation helps identify which modalities contribute most to performance and informs future fine-tuning and architecture choices.

In practical deployment, multimodal models often require specialized hardware to handle the increased complexity. Training multimodal LLMs on GPUs or TPUs is essential for handling the large-scale computations required by cross-modal attention mechanisms. Additionally, storage and memory demands are higher due to the need to process and retain different input types. Deploying multimodal LLMs often involves balancing the computational load across multiple servers or using dedicated hardware accelerators, especially for applications with real-time constraints.

By following the strategies outlined in this chapter, developers can build,

train, and deploy multimodal LLMs that seamlessly integrate text, images,

audio, and other data types. These models enable richer, more context-

aware applications that meet the demands of complex real-world

scenarios.

Implementing LLMs with Python and TensorFlow

Setting Up the Environment

To implement large language models, setting up the development environment is the first step.

- **Python and TensorFlow:** Install the necessary libraries and dependencies, including Python, TensorFlow, and other relevant packages.

- **Development Tools:** Use tools like Jupyter Notebooks for interactive development and debugging.

Data Preparation

Effective data preparation is key to successful model training.

- **Data Collection:** Gather and preprocess text data from diverse sources, ensuring it is representative and relevant.

- **Tokenization:** Tokenize the text into suitable units (words, subwords, or characters) and create the necessary input formats for the model.

Model Architecture and Implementation

Implementing the model architecture involves defining the layers and components of the LLM.

- **Transformer Architecture:** Use TensorFlow to build the Transformer model, including attention mechanisms, positional encodings, and multi-head attention layers.
- **Custom Layers:** Implement custom layers and functions as needed for specific tasks or improvements.

Training and Fine-Tuning an LLM

Train and fine-tune the model on the prepared data.

- **Training Loop:** Define the training loop, specifying the optimizer, learning rate, and loss function. Use techniques like learning rate scheduling and gradient clipping to enhance training stability.

- **Fine-Tuning:** Fine-tune the pre-trained model on task-specific data, adjusting hyperparameters and monitoring performance to achieve optimal results.

Evaluating Model Performance

Evaluating the model's performance ensures it meets the desired criteria.

- **Metrics:** Use evaluation metrics such as accuracy, F1 score, and perplexity to assess the model's performance on validation and test datasets.

- **Error Analysis:** Conduct error analysis to identify and address areas where the model may be underperforming, refining the model as necessary.

Advanced Techniques in LLMs

Transfer Learning in LLMs

Transfer learning is a powerful technique that leverages pre-trained models on large datasets and fine-tunes them on specific tasks or domains. This approach significantly reduces the amount of data and computational resources required for training.

- **Pre-Training:** Involves training an LLM on a vast corpus of text data to capture general language understanding.

- **Fine-Tuning:** Adapting the pre-trained model to specific tasks (e.g., sentiment analysis, text classification) by training it further on task-specific data.

Prompt Engineering

Prompt engineering involves designing effective input prompts to guide the model in generating desired outputs. This technique is especially useful for models like GPT-3 and GPT-4, which can perform various tasks based on the given prompts.

- **Crafting Prompts:** Creating clear and specific prompts to elicit accurate and relevant responses from the model.

- **Contextual Prompts:** Including context or examples in the prompt to improve the model's understanding and response quality.

Zero-Shot and Few-Shot Learning

Zero-shot and few-shot learning are techniques that enable models to perform tasks with little to no task-specific training data.

- **Zero-Shot Learning:** The model performs a task without having seen any examples of it during training, relying solely on its pre-trained knowledge.

- **Few-Shot Learning:** The model is given a few examples (usually between one and a handful) of the task during inference to understand and perform the task.

Scaling and Distributed Training

Scaling LLMs involves increasing the model size, data, and computational resources to improve performance. Distributed training techniques enable efficient training of large models across multiple GPUs or machines.

- **Model Parallelism:** Distributing different parts of the model across multiple devices.

- **Data Parallelism:** Splitting the training data across multiple devices and synchronizing model updates.

Applications and Use Cases

Natural Language Understanding

LLMs excel in understanding and interpreting human language, making them valuable for tasks such as:

- **Question Answering:** Providing accurate answers to user queries based on the context.
- **Named Entity Recognition:** Identifying entities like names, dates, and locations in text.
- **Text Classification:** Categorizing text into predefined labels.

Text Generation

Text generation involves creating coherent and contextually relevant text based on given input prompts.

- **Storytelling:** Generating creative stories or content.
- **Content Creation:** Assisting with writing articles, blog posts, and social media content.

Conversational AI and Chatbots

LLMs power conversational agents that can engage in human-like dialogues.

- **Customer Support:** Automating responses to common queries and providing assistance.

- **Virtual Assistants:** Helping users with tasks like scheduling, reminders, and information retrieval.

Sentiment Analysis and Opinion Mining

LLMs analyze text to determine the sentiment or emotion expressed.

- **Social Media Monitoring:** Understanding public sentiment towards brands, products, or events.

- **Customer Feedback Analysis:** Extracting insights from reviews and feedback.

Summarization and Translation

LLMs can summarize long documents into concise summaries and translate text between languages.

- **Document Summarization:** Condensing lengthy texts while preserving key information.

- **Language Translation:** Translating text with high accuracy across multiple languages.

Performance Optimization and Deployment

Optimizing Model Performance

Optimizing LLMs involves improving their efficiency and effectiveness.

- **Hyperparameter Tuning:** Adjusting hyperparameters like learning rate and batch size to enhance performance.
- **Regularization Techniques:** Applying techniques like dropout and weight decay to prevent overfitting.

Model Compression and Quantization

Model compression and quantization reduce the size and computational requirements of LLMs, making them more efficient.

- **Pruning:** Removing less important connections in the network to reduce model size.
- **Quantization:** Reducing the precision of model weights and activations to lower memory and computational costs.

Deploying LLMs in Production

Deploying LLMs involves setting up infrastructure to serve the models in real-world applications.

- **Inference Optimization:** Ensuring efficient and fast model inference
- **Scalability:** Designing systems that can handle high request volumes and scale as needed.

Monitoring and Maintenance

Continuous monitoring and maintenance ensure the deployed models remain effective and reliable.

- **Performance Monitoring:** Tracking model performance and detecting issues.
- **Regular Updates:** Updating models with new data and improvements to maintain accuracy and relevance.

Case Studies

Industry Use Cases

Exploring how LLMs are applied across different industries.

- **Healthcare:** Using LLMs for medical diagnosis and patient interaction.

- **Finance:** Automating customer service and analyzing financial documents.

Research Applications

LLMs in academic and scientific research.

- **Language Modeling:** Advancing the state-of-the-art in NLP research.

- **Knowledge Discovery:** Extracting insights from scientific literature.

- **Case Study 1: Healthcare - Enhancing Patient Interaction with AI-Assisted Diagnostics**

- A major healthcare provider sought to improve patient interaction and diagnostic accuracy by implementing an AI-assisted chatbot for initial consultations. Patients frequently had difficulty navigating complex medical information and understanding symptoms, which led to high volumes of routine questions and administrative strain on healthcare staff. The goal was to build a large language model capable of providing initial assessments, answering basic medical questions, and assisting patients with symptom tracking.

- **Implementation Strategy**

- To create the chatbot, the healthcare provider used a fine-tuned LLM trained on a combination of general medical literature, electronic health records (EHRs) (with personal identifiers removed for privacy), and symptom-based datasets. The model was integrated with a knowledge graph, which provided a structured understanding of medical terms, symptoms, and potential treatments. This multimodal setup allowed the chatbot to answer patient questions, assess initial symptoms, and recommend whether a patient should seek urgent care or book a regular appointment.

- **Challenges**

- The primary challenges were maintaining data privacy, ensuring diagnostic accuracy, and avoiding liability for incorrect recommendations. Privacy was managed by anonymizing all patient data and maintaining compliance with HIPAA. Ensuring the accuracy of the chatbot's recommendations was difficult, especially since medical language and patient symptoms can vary significantly. The team implemented a conservative approach where uncertain queries were escalated to a human healthcare provider, preventing risky autonomous recommendations.

- **Outcomes**

- The chatbot reduced routine inquiry volume by 40%, allowing staff to focus on critical cases. Additionally, patient satisfaction improved due to immediate assistance and symptom-tracking advice. While the model is limited to non-critical assessments, its deployment demonstrated the potential of LLMs in reducing administrative burdens and enhancing patient interaction in healthcare settings.

- **Case Study 2: Retail - Personalizing Customer Experience with AI-Powered Recommendations**
- An online retail company specializing in fashion faced increasing competition and sought to differentiate itself by improving customer experience through personalized recommendations. Existing recommendation systems were limited to analyzing purchase history, lacking the capability to respond to real-time customer interactions. The company aimed to create a language model that could interact with users in natural language and provide style advice and tailored product recommendations.
- **Implementation Strategy**
- The retailer trained a large language model on product descriptions, customer reviews, and past interactions to understand customer preferences. The LLM was integrated with the retailer's inventory database and combined with collaborative filtering techniques to provide personalized recommendations. Customers could interact

with a chatbot to discuss their style preferences, ask for specific clothing recommendations, and even seek outfit suggestions.

- **Challenges**

- Training the model to understand fashion terminology and subjective style preferences was challenging. Initial model outputs were too generic, so the team enhanced the training set with fashion blog data, trend reports, and style guides. Privacy was also a consideration, as personal customer data was used in training. To address this, customer consent was obtained, and data encryption protocols were enforced.

- **Outcomes**

- The retailer reported a 25% increase in conversion rates and a 35% improvement in customer satisfaction scores. The AI-driven style advisor became one of the site's most popular features, significantly enhancing customer loyalty. This case highlighted the impact of LLMs in enhancing personalized shopping experiences through interactive and context-aware customer engagement.

- **Case Study 3: Legal - Streamlining Contract Analysis for Law Firms**

- A prominent law firm faced challenges with the time-consuming task of contract analysis. Reviewing contracts manually took significant time, often leading to delayed client responses. The firm decided to implement an LLM to expedite the contract review process, particularly in identifying risk factors, non-standard clauses, and summarizing contractual obligations.

- **Implementation Strategy**

- The law firm trained the LLM on legal texts, contracts, and previously analyzed cases to identify key legal terms and patterns. By incorporating an attention mechanism focused on legalese, the model could highlight unusual clauses or potential red flags in contracts. It was designed to produce clause-specific summaries and flag high-risk terms for attorney review.

- **Challenges**

- The primary concern was the accuracy of the model, as minor errors could have serious legal implications. Additionally, ensuring client data security was critical, given the sensitive nature of legal documents. The firm took a cautious approach, deploying the model only in a supervised mode where it supplemented human analysis rather than replacing it. The model was regularly audited to verify the accuracy of its assessments.

- **Outcomes**

- The model reduced contract review time by 50%, freeing attorneys to focus on complex legal issues rather than routine contract analysis. Client feedback was positive, as response times improved significantly. The law firm's productivity saw a measurable increase, underscoring the utility of LLMs in enhancing efficiency in knowledge-driven sectors like law.

- **Case Study 4: Financial Services - Automating Loan Processing and Credit Scoring**
- A financial institution sought to automate its loan processing workflow, including initial credit scoring and document verification. Traditional processes relied heavily on manual evaluation, making it challenging to provide real-time loan assessments. The goal was to build an LLM that could assess loan applications and predict creditworthiness while adhering to regulatory standards.
- **Implementation Strategy**
- The LLM was fine-tuned on historical loan applications, customer financial data, and relevant economic indicators. It was integrated with a rules-based system to ensure compliance with lending standards. The model analyzed applicants' financial documents, employment history, and credit scores, making recommendations for approval or rejection based on predicted risk levels.
- **Challenges**

- The institution faced compliance and interpretability challenges. Regulations required transparency in credit scoring, meaning the model's decisions had to be explainable. To address this, the institution used a hybrid approach, combining the LLM with interpretable machine learning models for parts of the decision process. Security was also critical, so data encryption and anonymization measures were implemented.

- **Outcomes**

- The LLM reduced loan processing times by 60%, allowing the institution to approve loans within hours instead of days. Customer satisfaction improved, as did the bank's loan origination rate. The case demonstrated how LLMs can enhance decision-making processes in financial services, provided interpretability and compliance are prioritized.

- **Case Study 5: Education - Personalized Tutoring with AI-Driven Feedback**

- An online education platform aimed to enhance student engagement by providing AI-driven tutoring support. With thousands of students on the platform, offering personalized feedback was a challenge. The platform decided to develop an LLM that could evaluate students' responses, provide feedback, and suggest improvement areas for writing, comprehension, and problem-solving skills.

- **Implementation Strategy**

- The education platform trained the LLM on a diverse set of academic texts, student submissions, and grading rubrics. The model was designed to evaluate essays, generate feedback, and recommend resources. It could assess grammar, structure, and coherence in writing assignments, providing suggestions tailored to each student's learning level.

- **Challenges**

- Ensuring accuracy in feedback was critical, as incorrect advice could mislead students. Additionally, the platform had to address potential biases in the model, particularly in scoring students from different backgrounds. Regular evaluations of feedback quality and adjustments to prevent bias were implemented. Privacy was also a concern, as student data had to be protected under educational privacy laws.

- **Outcomes**

- The LLM increased student engagement by 30% and improved learning outcomes, as students benefited from instant, constructive feedback. Teachers were able to focus more on curriculum planning rather than grading, and the platform saw a boost in subscriptions. This case highlighted how LLMs can support personalized learning experiences in education, provided there is ongoing quality control and bias mitigation.

Real-World Implementations

Showcasing successful implementations of LLMs in real-world scenarios.

- **Customer Support:** Enhancing customer service experiences.
- **Content Generation:** Automating content creation for marketing and media.

Future of Large Language Models

Trends and Innovations

Exploring the latest trends and innovations in LLM research and development.

- **Advancements in Architecture:** New model architectures and techniques.
- **Integration with Other Technologies:** Combining LLMs with other AI technologies.

Challenges and Opportunities

Identifying the challenges and opportunities in the field of LLMs.

- **Ethical and Social Implications:** Addressing concerns related to bias, fairness, and privacy.

- **Scalability and Efficiency:** Improving the scalability and efficiency of LLMs.

The Role of LLMs in AI Research

Discussing the impact of LLMs on AI research and their future potential.

- **Driving Innovation:** How LLMs are pushing the boundaries of AI research.

- **Future Directions:** Potential future developments and research directions.

Hands-On Projects and Exercises

Project 1: Building a Text Generator

Step-by-step guide to creating a text generator using an LLM.

- **Data Preparation:** Collecting and preprocessing text data.

- **Model Implementation:** Building and training the text generation model.

- **Evaluation:** Assessing the generated text quality.

Project 2: Creating a Chatbot with LLM

Developing a conversational AI chatbot.

- **Designing Conversations:** Creating dialogue flows and responses.

- **Training the Chatbot:** Fine-tuning the LLM for conversational tasks.

- **Deployment:** Deploying the chatbot and integrating with user interfaces.

Project 3: Sentiment Analysis Using LLM

Implementing a sentiment analysis system.

- **Data Collection:** Gathering labeled sentiment data.

- **Model Training:** Training the LLM for sentiment classification.

- **Evaluation and Tuning:** Optimizing and evaluating model performance.

Project 4: Automated Text Summarization

Creating a text summarization system.

- **Data Preparation:** Collecting and preprocessing documents.

- **Model Implementation:** Building the summarization model.

- **Evaluation:** Assessing the quality of generated summaries.

Project 5: Translating Text with LLM

Developing a language translation system.

- **Data Collection:** Gathering parallel text data for training.

- **Model Training:** Training the LLM for translation tasks.

- **Evaluation:** Evaluating translation quality and accuracy.

Project 1: Building a Text Generator

Solution:

1. **Data Preparation:**

   ○ Collect a large corpus of text data from sources like Wikipedia, books, or web articles.

   ○ Preprocess the data by cleaning, tokenizing, and converting it into a suitable format for training.

2. **Model Implementation:**

   ○ Use the transformers library from Hugging Face.

   ○ Load a pre-trained model like GPT-3 or GPT-4.

   ○ Fine-tune the model on your dataset.

python

Copy code

```
from transformers import GPT2LMHeadModel, GPT2Tokenizer, TextDataset, DataCollatorForLanguageModeling, Trainer, TrainingArguments


# Load pre-trained model and tokenizer
model = GPT2LMHeadModel.from_pretrained('gpt2')

tokenizer = GPT2Tokenizer.from_pretrained('gpt2')
```

```python
# Prepare the dataset
def load_dataset(file_path, tokenizer):
    dataset = TextDataset(
        tokenizer=tokenizer,
        file_path=file_path,
        block_size=128
    )
    return dataset


dataset = load_dataset('path/to/your/text/data.txt', tokenizer)
data_collator = DataCollatorForLanguageModeling(tokenizer=tokenizer,
mlm=False)


# Fine-tune the model
training_args = TrainingArguments(
    output_dir='./results',
    overwrite_output_dir=True,
    num_train_epochs=1,
    per_device_train_batch_size=4,
```

```python
    save_steps=10_000,

    save_total_limit=2,

)


trainer = Trainer(

    model=model,

    args=training_args,

    data_collator=data_collator,

    train_dataset=dataset,

)


trainer.train()
```

3. **Evaluation:**

   o Generate text using the fine-tuned model and evaluate its quality.

python

Copy code

```python
input_text = "Once upon a time"
```

```python
inputs = tokenizer(input_text, return_tensors='pt')

outputs = model.generate(inputs['input_ids'], max_length=100,
num_return_sequences=1)


print(tokenizer.decode(outputs[0], skip_special_tokens=True))
```

Project 2: Creating a Chatbot with LLM

Solution:

1. **Designing Conversations:**

   o Define dialogue flows and responses.

   o Prepare a dataset of conversational pairs.

2. **Training the Chatbot:**

   o Fine-tune a conversational model like DialoGPT on your conversational dataset.

python

Copy code

```python
from transformers import AutoModelForCausalLM, AutoTokenizer,
Trainer, TrainingArguments
```

```python
# Load pre-trained conversational model and tokenizer
model = AutoModelForCausalLM.from_pretrained("microsoft/DialoGPT-medium")
tokenizer = AutoTokenizer.from_pretrained("microsoft/DialoGPT-medium")


# Prepare the conversational dataset
dataset = load_dataset('path/to/your/conversational/data.txt', tokenizer)
data_collator = DataCollatorForLanguageModeling(tokenizer=tokenizer, mlm=False)


# Fine-tune the model
trainer = Trainer(
    model=model,
    args=training_args,
    data_collator=data_collator,
    train_dataset=dataset,
)
```

```
trainer.train()
```

3. **Deployment:**

   o Integrate the chatbot with user interfaces like a web app or messaging platform.

python

Copy code

```
# Example of a simple interactive chatbot loop
while True:
    input_text = input("User: ")
    inputs = tokenizer.encode(input_text + tokenizer.eos_token, return_tensors='pt')
    outputs = model.generate(inputs, max_length=1000, pad_token_id=tokenizer.eos_token_id)
    response = tokenizer.decode(outputs[:, inputs.shape[-1]:][0], skip_special_tokens=True)
    print(f"Chatbot: {response}")
```

Project 3: Sentiment Analysis Using LLM

Solution:

1. **Data Collection:**

   ○ Gather labeled sentiment data, e.g., from movie reviews or social media.

2. **Model Training:**

   ○ Fine-tune a pre-trained sentiment analysis model like BERT on your dataset.

python

Copy code

```python
from transformers import BertTokenizer, BertForSequenceClassification, Trainer, TrainingArguments
from datasets import load_dataset


# Load pre-trained BERT model and tokenizer
model = BertForSequenceClassification.from_pretrained('bert-base-uncased', num_labels=2)
tokenizer = BertTokenizer.from_pretrained('bert-base-uncased')


# Load and prepare the sentiment dataset
```

```python
dataset = load_dataset('csv', data_files={'train':
'path/to/your/sentiment/data.csv'})

dataset = dataset.map(lambda e: tokenizer(e['text'], truncation=True,
padding='max_length'), batched=True)

dataset.set_format(type='torch', columns=['input_ids', 'attention_mask',
'label'])


# Fine-tune the model

training_args = TrainingArguments(

    output_dir='./results',

    overwrite_output_dir=True,

    num_train_epochs=3,

    per_device_train_batch_size=8,

    save_steps=10_000,

    save_total_limit=2,

)


trainer = Trainer(

    model=model,
```

```python
    args=training_args,

    train_dataset=dataset['train'],

)
```

trainer.train()

3. **Evaluation and Tuning:**

   ○ Evaluate the model's accuracy and fine-tune as necessary.

python

Copy code

```python
# Example of predicting sentiment

input_text = "I love this product!"

inputs = tokenizer(input_text, return_tensors='pt')

outputs = model(**inputs)

predictions = torch.argmax(outputs.logits, dim=-1)

sentiment = 'positive' if predictions[0].item() == 1 else 'negative'

print(f"Sentiment: {sentiment}")
```

Project 4: Automated Text Summarization

Solution:

1. **Data Preparation:**

   ○ Collect and preprocess documents for summarization.

2. **Model Implementation:**

   ○ Use a pre-trained summarization model like T5.

python

Copy code

```python
from transformers import T5ForConditionalGeneration, T5Tokenizer


# Load pre-trained T5 model and tokenizer

model = T5ForConditionalGeneration.from_pretrained('t5-small')

tokenizer = T5Tokenizer.from_pretrained('t5-small')


# Prepare the dataset

input_text = "summarize: " + "Your document text goes here."

inputs = tokenizer.encode(input_text, return_tensors='pt', max_length=512, truncation=True)


# Generate the summary
```

```python
summary_ids = model.generate(inputs, max_length=150, min_length=40,
length_penalty=2.0, num_beams=4, early_stopping=True)
summary = tokenizer.decode(summary_ids[0], skip_special_tokens=True)

print(f"Summary: {summary}")
```

3. **Evaluation:**

   ◦ Assess the quality of summaries and fine-tune the model if necessary.

Project 5: Translating Text with LLM

Solution:

1. **Data Collection:**

   ◦ Gather parallel text data for training (e.g., English-French translations).

2. **Model Training:**

   ◦ Use a pre-trained translation model like MarianMT.

python

Copy code

```python
from transformers import MarianMTModel, MarianTokenizer

# Load pre-trained MarianMT model and tokenizer
model_name = 'Helsinki-NLP/opus-mt-en-fr'
model = MarianMTModel.from_pretrained(model_name)
tokenizer = MarianTokenizer.from_pretrained(model_name)

# Translate text
input_text = "How are you?"
inputs = tokenizer.encode(input_text, return_tensors='pt')

# Generate translation
translated_ids = model.generate(inputs, max_length=40, num_beams=4,
early_stopping=True)
translation                  =                  tokenizer.decode(translated_ids[0],
skip_special_tokens=True)

print(f"Translation: {translation}")
```

3. **Evaluation:**

o   Evaluate translation quality and refine the model as needed.

www.ingramcontent.com/pod-product-compliance
Lightning Source LLC
LaVergne TN
LVHW051605050326
832903LV00033B/4376